I0532432

Living
RESILIENTLY

*Black, Blind and Female
The Journey Continues*

Kari Kelley BEST SELLING AUTHOR,
SPEAKER & INSPIRATIONAL LEADER

Living Resiliently!
Black, Blind, and Female: The Journey Continues

Copyright © 2023 by Kari Kelley

Photo by James Adams-James Adams Photography
Make up by Forever Cosmetics
Jewelry by Cassandra F. Garabedian A chest of Jewels

RHG Media Productions
25495 Southwick Drive #103
Hayward, CA 94544.

All rights reserved. No part of this publication may be reproduced distributed or transmitted in any form or by any means including photocopying recording or other electronic or mechanical means without proper written permission of author or publisher, except in the case of brief quotations embodied in critical reviews and certain other noncommercial uses permitted by copyright law.

ISBN 979-8-9878577-0-0 (paperback)
ISBN 979-8-9878577-1-7 (hardcover)

Printed in the United States of America.

What People Are Saying

"This book is an amazing, inspiring journey, where bitter lemons of life turn into delicious lemonade of life-changing experiences… I recommend this book to anyone who is ready for a life change, and freedom!"
-Toni Stone Bruce, Founder & CEO Precious Stones 4 Life, LLC
Motivational speaker, Best-seller international author, health & wellness consultant

"A powerful, beautiful guide on how to build a resilient life, one choice at a time."
-Marlene Elizabeth, Certified Positive Intelligence® Coach
Moneywings™ Retreats for Entrepreneurs

"This book is powerful beyond words."
-Rosalyn Kahn, Coaching and Professional Speaking

"Living Resiliently is a heroic story of emerging victorious over odds, narrated in a deeply moving manner... Living Resiliently is a masterpiece that exudes inspiration."
-Atifa Deshamukhya, Certified Life Coach (ICF)
Director, Aspiring Excellence Private Limited

"Living Resiliently! ~Black, Blind, and Female: The Journey Continues~ is a compelling book that encourages you as the reader, to live resiliently!"
-Cynthia Stott, International Speech and Confidence Coach, Global Visibility Influencer

"Kelley's intent is to provide actionable steps to heal and grow stronger, overcoming life's challenges."
-James Adams, Master Photographer
Photographic Craftsman

"From the first sentence, I knew this book was one of spirituality and healing, and I was drawn to that immediately."
-Carolyn CJ Jones, Gold-medal-winning Author for Self-help Spirituality
Motivational Speaker, Forgiveness Coach, Registered Nurse (Ret.)

"This book is an amazing read! Kari Kelley pulled at my heartstrings as she shared her story of the challenges she has faced throughout her life."

-Lydia Norman, Disability Advocate and Public Speaker

"Kari shows us what it means to be resilient - to clear hurdles, obstacles, difficulties, challenges.
This book is the need of the hour."

-Dr. Mary Thomas, Medical Doctor, Motivational Speaker, International Best-Selling Author

Contents

CHAPTER ONE

What is Living Resiliently?

I believe that living resiliently is the ability to access healing as you are experiencing adversity. Being a black, legally blind, woman living in the United States, I am convinced that being resilient for me is the one thing that allows me to survive. As I follow current events, I can easily be tempted to pull the covers over my head, curl into the fetal position, and stay there indefinitely. I am convinced that it is my resilience, along with the presence of three little girls in the bedroom next to mine, that propels me to uncurl myself, kick off those blankets, and plant my feet on the floor. As I share my personal experiences with resilience, I encourage you to recognize your own resilience and tap into it so that you can be strong. **The human condition presents all of us with challenges. It is our resilience**

that sustains us as we face them. Our body has built-in healing abilities, and modern medicine can boost the healing process as needed. Mental resilience is our ability to tame our thoughts and/ or shift our beliefs. Spiritual resilience is also built in. The spirit is the force that provides stabilization above and beyond what is physical and mental; however, it directly affects both.

My three-year-old granddaughter is the best example of resilience on all three levels, mental, physical, and spiritual. A good demonstration is the "kiss it and make it all better." Whenever she falls down and the slightest scrape, bump, or bruise shows up, part of treating the wound is to "kiss it and make it all better." She almost immediately stops crying and in less than five minutes goes right back to running and jumping or doing whatever she was doing that originally caused the fall. For a short time after, the scrape, bump, or bruise is shown off as a badge of honor, and the entire story of how it happened is told with dramatic flair and the expansive vocabulary that a three-year-old is capable of. Her physical resilience will heal the scrape, bump, or bruise over time. A quick wash-off and a Band-Aid will get the job done.

Her mind is made up that a kiss makes a hurt feel better. I found this out when I was playing with her and I banged my knee.

"Ouch!" I said as I rubbed my knee.

"What happened?" she asked.

"I banged my knee," I said.

She said, "I'll kiss it."

So here I am at a place where I can either let her kiss it and allow her to go on thinking that a kiss will make it better or shift her belief by explaining that it will take more than a kiss to make the pain go away. For the record, I let her kiss it.

Mental resilience can be a bit more challenging than the "kiss it and make it all better" that works for the three-year-old. Taming the wild thoughts that present themselves for occupying mind space can be challenging. The energy they bring with them is where mental resilience matters. When my wild thoughts dwell on the adversity I may encounter when I leave my safe space, I feel fear and sadness and frustration. Then the downward spiral begins. My feelings of fear, sadness, and frustration produce more thoughts of doom and gloom and so it goes.

The good news is that just like the way a downward spiral can start, all it takes is for a thought of positivity to present itself for occupying mind space. Once that positive thought is in place, more of its friends can join it. Then the spark of joy turns into a flame of happiness and the energy begins to lighten up. I believe that spiritual resilience is the cause of the positive thought that shows up when it is needed the most.

This book shows that resilience is available not just physically but also mentally and spiritually. Whatever called to you from this book... I am committed to providing both inspiration and practical ways to access your own built-in resilience. **As an adult survivor of childhood abuse, I share recognition of my own resilience and model it for other survivors. It has been said that hurt people hurt other** people. However, I believe that healing people also heal other people, and this is what compels me to share my healing journey so that others can heal.

I am committed to providing resources that will allow you, the reader, to recognize how you have already been resilient and how you can focus on the light and use it to guide you. Each chapter will contain Resilient Living Tips. These tips are designed for you to actively recognize, celebrate, and share your resilience. In this book, you will learn where to search for your resilience. You will be eager to celebrate your resilience. That celebration will attract opportunities to connect with more resilience in the form of more healing for yourself and others. **Resilience is like light. No matter how dark it is, the smallest spark lights the place where it is shining. No matter how long it has been dark, the light eventually shines.**

You are still breathing; know that you are resilient. I am glad you are reading this book because it means that you are interested in Living Resiliently.

Resilient Living Tips

1. Make a list of any physical scrapes, bumps, and bruises that are still in the healing process. Consider what you may need to do in order to boost the body's ability to continue to heal and take those actions.

2. Is there an action/mindset that you can take on that will help the healing process? Your own "kiss" to make it better? (I'm sending positive energy and support to remind you that you are not alone; your hurts matter and are cared for.)

3. Know that you can choose to turn them into a badge of honor and a testament to what you have survived. A reminder of your RESILIENCE.

Notes

_____

_____

_____

_____

_____

_____

_____

_____

_____

_____

_____

_____

_____

_____

_____

_____

_____

_____

_____

_____

_____

Notes

_____

_____

_____

_____

_____

_____

_____

_____

_____

_____

_____

_____

_____

_____

_____

_____

_____

_____

_____

_____

_____

CHAPTER TWO

The Past

I remember my fourth birthday in some detail. I was in foster care at the time. My foster mother was explaining to me that I was four years old because it was my birthday.

"But I'm three," I said.

"Today you are four," she said.

I put my four-year-old hands on my four-year-old hips and stomped my four-year-old foot and proclaimed in no uncertain terms, "I'm three!"

My birthday is in January, and I was adopted in April to what turned out to be my second new family. I was adopted the first time when I was nine months old. During my first adoption, I was shaken and my head was banged while I was being shaken. It took about ten days for me to receive medical attention. This abuse left me legally blind. I was removed and placed in foster care. The abuse I would experience in my second new family started on the drive away from my foster home as I cried uncontrollably in the back seat of the car my new daddy was driving. My new mother turned around in the front seat and pointed her finger at me.

"You shut up all that noise!" she yelled.

I understood right away that I better shut right up. I stayed quiet for years. I stayed quiet while my mother told me how ugly, stupid, and good for nothing I was. I stayed quiet while she told me that I should be grateful that anyone adopted me because no one wants a half-blind, ugly, stupid child with crooked teeth and nappy hair. I desperately tried to stay quiet when she dragged a comb without mercy through my thick, coarse hair. If I didn't stay quiet, a slap was forthcoming along with her angry words like, "I'll give you something to cry about" or "Shut up! I'm not hurting you!" I stayed quiet when my mother said that she loved her grandchildren more than she loved me. She never failed to act that out.

For example, she bought them brand new clothes, and I got clothes from other family members or a used clothing store. I stayed quiet while being introduced to sexual information immediately after joining my new family. I stayed quiet about being raped when I was eight.

Have you stayed silent about something? Is it time to release the silence from the past and move forward?

My mother had a stroke when I was ten years old. This left her paralyzed on her right side and confined to a wheelchair. Before the stroke, my mother was very independent. Losing her independence caused her to become bitter. She did maintain some of her independence by continuing to cook and having a candy store in our living room. I became a caregiver for her and took on more household responsibilities. During the summer of my thirteenth birthday, my mother went into the hospital and my father dropped me off with relatives. This had been the norm ever since my mother had the stroke. He always picked me up when she came home. This particular hospital stay would be her last. My cousin woke me up in the wee hours to tell me my mother had died. My father never picked me back up. I stayed with relatives through the eighth and ninth grades, going "home" on the weekends.

I had much more freedom at "home" than I did at my relative's house. I found a way to move back home. But the freedom I gained cost me dearly. You see, the relationship with my father was great until I was twelve. For years, I had dealt with sexual abuse from other people, but I thought my father was safe. So, when he woke me up by trying to get in bed with me (when I was just twelve years old), my first thought was he must be drunk. However, he was not drunk, but he left my room as I made my voice loud enough for my mother to overhear. I waited for my mother to say something, but she never talked to me. Instead, she called other family members and told them. Years later, when I moved in with him, I knew that having sex with him was part of the deal. When living with my father became too overwhelming, I moved back in with relatives. When it became overwhelming to live with relatives, I moved back with my father. The moving and overwhelm took a toll, and on Father's Day 1987, I tried to end my life. I spent seventy-two hours in the psych ward at Stanford Children's hospital. I was seventeen at the time. After I got out, I went right back to my father's house until he got married. I lived with him and his new wife until they moved away. I couldn't go with them because I was still in high school. I didn't graduate with my class due to all of the classes I had skipped and flunked. Instead, I graduated one year later. But this is the past. I share it with you so you know where I have come from and what I was able to rise above. I have discovered our past does not dictate our future. We cannot undo or choose what has happened to us in the past, but we can choose to rise above and build a life and future that matters to us. **I was able, like the Phoenix, to rise again...I discovered my resilience. You too can rise above. You too can tap into your resilience no matter what has happened in the past. You can choose to move forward.** What are you willing to rise above...what is no longer serving you that you are willing to release? So that you can step forward and be and become all that you desire to be?

During the time I was experiencing all this, I couldn't find a silver lining. I believe it is the rare gifted person who can find the silver lining in the midst of a crisis or trauma. It took me some time to recognize the silver lining(s) that were present during the years. In fact, some silver linings were not visible to me because I had no idea they existed. I was forty-two years old when I realized that my fourteen-month-old body was created stronger than average so that when I was shaken, my injuries didn't kill me. And my head was just a little harder than the average so that all I lost was some of my eyesight. As I reminisce about my childhood, I am reminded of some of the people in my new family that were good to me. Although I was teased in school, I did have some friends. There were teachers and people at church who I know loved me. I also discovered I have a strong survival instinct and that I am resilient. I will rise again and again. I have and will heal, love, and live positively and powerfully.

Navigating my life with limited eyesight is a challenge; however, I believe eyesight and vision are different. Eyesight is what one can see as one of the physical senses, and vision is what the spirit contributes to one's heart. My eyesight looks at an empty room. However, my vision creates a fully decorated room with my favorite colors with the furniture placed just the way I want it. During my childhood, being legally blind had its ups and downs. I was taken to many doctors to "get my eyes fixed." I had special training to learn to do things like cooking and shopping, while using special devices. When it came time for me to learn how to cross the street, I had to use my ears rather than my eyes to know when it was safe for me to cross. Since driving a car was not in my future, I made housing choices based on the location of how far I would have to carry things like groceries and laundry. Convincing employers that I could be a productive employee once accommodations were made was not the easiest, but I was able to work in the corporate world for almost seventeen years.

Being legally blind has enhanced my other senses. I have also learned how to advocate for myself to ask for what I need. Being legally blind allows me a level of freedom that shields me from seeing some things that I am happy not to see, such as injuries that may be visible from a car accident and disturbing news footage. I have been blessed to see a rainbow and the smiling faces of children. My vision paints pictures that are full of color. My vision is fueling my efforts to share my story of resilience every chance I get so that I contribute to keeping a child safe from abuse. My vision shows me a person who was so inspired by my story that he or she made a choice to take action on behalf of a child that they knew was in harm's way. In my vision, I am surrounded by children who grew up to be well-adjusted adults because of the work I am doing today that makes that future possible.

Moving Forward/Choice

I realize that the present moment is a gift. When I reflect on my past, I am very sure and very clear that I was specifically created for the challenges that came my way. My head was just hard enough not to be completely crushed from the head injury that I sustained at fourteen months old. My body was just a little stronger than the average in order to withstand shaken baby syndrome. Statistics show that not every fourteen-month-old child lives through either of these situations; I survived both.

Today, I am grateful for my life. I was not always happy and joyful about being alive. For some time during my late teens and early twenties, I kept wondering why I was still alive. I would wake up and be disappointed that I had to get through another day. I would spend that day doing reckless things with the belief that I was not going to live much longer. Gradually, my mindset shifted. Gaining my independence was the first turning point. Having my first apartment that I had to be responsible for gave me a reason to keep working. Then my relationships kept me hopeful. My desire for something more fueled my actions. First it was wanting to live closer to my job so I had to find another apartment. Whenever the relationships didn't work out, I wanted something to fill that emptiness. A few different religions did the job temporarily. Through all of that, I have learned that nothing takes the place of self-love. Self-love is also a process. **My process started with me looking at myself in the mirror and saying, "Today, I love you."**

Resilient Living Tips

1. Look at yourself in the mirror and say: "Today, I love you."

2. You no longer have to stay silent.

3. Choose to heal.

4. Release what does not serve.

5. Embrace your resilience.

Notes

Notes

_____

_____

_____

_____

_____

_____

_____

_____

_____

_____

_____

_____

_____

_____

_____

_____

_____

_____

_____

_____

_____

_____

CHAPTER THREE

Shame, Truth, and Strength

S hame is like the slow, steady coil of a boa constrictor snake that rhythmically wraps itself around you until it completely constricts your movements and chokes the breath right out of you. I began to experience shame after I was adopted at four. The first shame I remember feeling was being teased about my teeth not being straight. So, whenever I laughed, I put my hand over my mouth. Another feeling of shame that I remember quite early in life was never wanting to look directly at people. I spent more time looking down than anywhere else. I felt shame about the color of my skin. I felt shame about the texture of my hair. These were all things that I had no control over, yet I felt shame.

There was much public shaming at school and at church because I found myself having to do a lot of reading aloud. Being blind in one eye and struggling to see clearly with just my second eye, I could not see small print so that was a struggle at church. At school, I had to go up to the chalkboard to read what the teacher had written so people pointed and made comments and told me that I was in their way. There was shame about the way I dressed at school. There was shame around having to wear wigs sometimes to church and school. There just never seemed to be an end to the shame that I was constantly feeling. Added to this shame was what came as I carried the secret of sexual abuse that I was dealing with, and you have the makings of a very unhappy person.

I was constantly told how stupid I was, so when bad grades came home from school, it was a self-fulfilling prophecy. More shame. I was constantly told how ugly I was. So, during my teenage years, if a boy actually showed a little bit of interest, it never surprised me when he said things like, "Don't tell anyone you're my girlfriend." More shame. During the time I spent in the corporate world, I felt lots of shame for not having a college education. More shame.

I found navigating spiritual communities shameful when I didn't fit in with the group of women chatting about being happy homemakers and raising children, or the high-powered corporate executive assistant working and supporting high-powered executives in the workplace. I had none of that; I felt more shame.

What brought me so much joy turned into a shameful experience that had me wanting to let go of my gift. As a Pentecostal gospel singer, there is a level of singing that comes from deep within. It is a large sound and I had it; it was such a beautiful release for me to sing for people and give them everything. Then I started hearing things like, "Can you tone it down." I told God that I would not sing any more. I even asked Him to take away the gift of singing. I even stopped singing for a while. More shame.

As I look back over my life, I can see very clearly where I let my feelings of shame really take away my life and living it fully. There were days I would come home from work on a Friday and climb into bed and not get up until Monday morning when it was time to go back to work. There were times I would get completely dressed and be ready to go do something fun and social. Then my hand would touch the doorknob and I would feel as if I did not deserve to have fun or be social, so I would take those clothes off, get right back into bed, and stay there. I can even see now how shame had a large effect on my romantic relationships. Sometimes I stayed with people who were not treating me well because I thought that was all I deserved. There were times I walked away from beautiful relation-ships because I just knew that issue was going to drop, so I had better end it before I got hurt. Shame and low self-esteem clouded my ability to recog-nize insecurity and mistake it for unconditional love. I thought when he said he wanted me all to himself that was validation that I was very special. What it actually turned out to be was the con-trolling nature of someone who is very insecure.

The truth of being able to SHINE requires finding your truth and recognizing you have been on a journey leading to this moment and time, and that you now get to choose what you truly want to bring forward.

Looking back now, I can see how there was always a tiny spark of truth that struggled in the darkness of all of the shame, trying to swallow it up. The truth was in the laughing in spite of having to put my hand over my mouth. I am glad that I was able to laugh and smile anyway versus losing the ability to laugh and smile at all.

I no longer feel the need or the inclination to look down instead of directly at people. I also have no qualms about telling people that I am legally blind. Now I can be truly who I am and looking myself in the eye is the most important thing I do. As for my skin color and the texture of my hair, it is what it is. I did manage to get braces in my twenties, so I no longer put my hand over my mouth when I laugh or smile. I now know that I am not stupid and I am not ugly. I was not stupid or ugly back then; the difference is back then, I believed I was both stupid and ugly. Today I may not be a beauty queen and I may not have a college degree, but I know that I am not stupid or ugly. I think I am beautifully intelligent in my own way as are you.

As for me "toning down" the way, I sing and telling God to take away my gift, I have apologized and asked for forgiveness and now my houseplants love my voice. I can sing as loud as I want to for them and they never complain. I grew up singing in church. The first time I led a song in church, I was eight years old. That was the first time everyone in church was impressed and complimentary to me. As a result, gospel music is my feel-good music. I now sing gospel for church events and other occasions when I can sing gospel as opposed to secular music. I did branch out to singing R&B during my twenties and thirties with a live band. My first few shows in nightclubs had me feeling like a fish out of water because as much as I was used to singing for a crowd, I was not used to the seductive clothes or the ways I had to dance. As time went by, I became comfortable enough to be a front woman. Other special occasions I was able to share my gift include singing the national anthem for a minor league baseball team, outdoor festivals, weddings, funerals, and adding singing to my public speaking and my one-woman shows. **I have discovered how to turn the rejections I have experienced in life into stepping stones.** For those who rejected me because I was not like everybody else, I now wear my differences like a badge of honor today. I am truly grateful for the people here who have embraced me and accepted me.

I encourage you to embrace and celebrate your uniqueness. Know that you are beautifully, uniquely, and wonderfully made. I have experienced a level of unconditional love that I never thought was possible for me. I never had children of my own so I didn't understand a mother-child bond. When I became an instant grandmother through marriage, I fell in love with my grandchildren and I felt called to protect, love, and encourage my grandchildren. There is some truth to the bumper sticker that says, "If I had known how much fun grandchildren were, I would have had them first." Since these three little girls have come into my life, I have experienced a deep level of unconditional love, especially from the youngest one. She was six weeks old when she came to live with us. She is now three and her level of unconditional love, wanting to be held and picked up, or spending time with me when I am at my worst, sometimes has shown me what a child can bring into one's life. The level of joy is completely off the charts. If I had only known what my life had in store for me back when I was carrying around the shame of being me. The spark of strength and truth and love has finally grown into a raging flame of self-love that I share with these three little girls. I am compelled by them and what their future will hold for them. I am committed to helping them never feel the kind of shame I grew up with and carried with me for a long time. Instead, I hope they continue to carry forward their beautiful, unconditional love of others and the celebration of who they are and how they are made.

Success is a moving target. When I was so wrapped up in shame, success was measured by what time it was, or if I could get out of bed. On a good day, I could get up at about noon. Then success was measured by how much time I could spend alone. Now I measure success by how many ways I can share my story of resilience. I believe that I will be successful by how many times someone makes the choice to put the safety of a child above and beyond anything else. I dream of hearing from countless people about how they heard my story and chose to put a child first. That is the success I am interested in. How are you defining success?

One way I found for me to break free of some of the shame I carried was to put my well-being first. Once I became clear that I had nothing to be ashamed of, that the abuse was not my fault, I chose to instead focus on what makes me feel good in a moment. When my mind takes me on a journey about wanting the people who abused me to hurt, I can think of all kinds of creative ways that they should pay for what they did. I also want all of the people that know I was being mistreated and abused and said nothing to pay as well. If I allow my mind to wander too far down this black hole, I end up feeling angry and bitter. This is where I have to remember what Nelson Mandala said,

"Holding on to bitterness is like you drinking poison, expecting someone else to die."

None of those people are losing any sleep over what they did to me. So, I choose to hurt and suffer less, even though I am wounded. I choose to release revenge, the desire to have people pay for what they did, and I choose instead to release this desire and move forward, echoing out the things that matter most to me. That creates the legacy I want for myself and my granddaughters. So, when I am feeling wounded, I find something that will make me feel better. Singing is usually a good place to start. Sometimes I will hear the laughter of the girls and that will effortlessly put a smile on my face. Your resilience is available on three levels - physically, mentally, and spiritually. If you focus on how you have healed on these levels, you will see your resilience.

Resilient Living Tips

1. Stand in your truth.

2. Differences are actually gifts to celebrate and share.

3. Don't "tone yourself down"; in fact, "Tone Yourself Up!"

4. Release the SHAME.

5. Find your purpose and reason to shine!

6. Choose how you define success.

7. Choose to SHINE by sharing how you have healed.

Notes

_____

_____

_____

_____

_____

_____

_____

_____

_____

_____

_____

_____

_____

_____

_____

_____

_____

_____

_____

_____

_____

Notes

_____

_____

_____

_____

_____

_____

_____

_____

_____

_____

_____

_____

_____

_____

_____

_____

_____

_____

_____

_____

_____

_____

CHAPTER FOUR

The Now

I had the belief that I would be a horrible mother. I also believed that if I did get pregnant, I would probably have to raise the baby alone. I felt that being legally blind would stop me from keeping my child safe. I just lived there in the land of paranoia, imagining all of the worst things that might happen to my child.

Based on my own childhood experiences, I made disparaging comments about parents who could not get their children to behave in public. I would shake my head and think about what happened to me when I was "that age." I knew many adults that held a tight rein on me and other children I knew. "I wouldn't dare act like that" or "my mother would kill me if I did that." I have since learned tolerance.

As I sit reflecting on what my life looks like today, it is very strange. When I think of my life when I was twenty years old and then thirty years old and even when I was forty years old, those times would never have given me the idea that my life would be the way it is right now. By the time I turned twenty, I was very clear that I didn't want children of my own. I was not very interested in a long-term relationship with anyone who had kids of their own. I couldn't see my place in a blended family. Once I turned thirty, however, I began to feel that I wouldn't find a man who didn't already have children, so I needed to figure out how to be in a blended family.

There is a bumper sticker that says, "If I had known how much fun grandchildren were, I would have had them first." I happened to fall in love with a man who had children of his own, and today I have three little girls in my life who have brought me a level of happiness and joy that I never would have thought was possible. I love the fact that I get to be a grandma without ever having children. I am so good at being a grandmother. Friends and family look at me and shake their heads because my behavior toward children is dramatically different nowadays. Now when I see a child having a tantrum, I have more compassion for the parents. I smile and wave at toddlers and say how cute they are. I speak to parents pushing strollers and inquire about due dates when I meet a pregnant woman.

First of all, I think they are the most beautiful girls to ever grace the earth, and I am fiercely protective. I found myself on a steep learning curve when my family moved in with us. The youngest girl was six weeks old, and I could not stand to hear her cry. Every little peep and whimper had me running to see what was wrong. It took a while for me to decipher which cry was one of distress and the cry of "I'm not getting my way right now this minute." The other two girls were four and eight when they moved in. The four-year-old and I bonded over shoes. She took one look at my shoe rack and tried to walk in the highest heels she could find. I held her hands and walked backwards, and we laughed while she wobbled around the house. My eight-year-old granddaughter is a talker. She has very firm opinions that she is always ready to defend.

I've spent a lot of time comparing them to myself when I was four and eight, and I love the carefree spirits that the girls have as compared to how shut down I was. I love telling them stories about old telephones and televisions that didn't have remote controls or a million channels. The looks of disbelief they give me is priceless. I love watching my husband be the best grandpa. It's hard to tell which one of us spoils the girls the most. As they get older, their preferences flip-flop between us. As I watch them grow, I feel like it's happening way too fast. I am filled with amazement and pride. It is so beautiful for me to see two loving parents keeping their children safe. I love watching the girls run to their dad when he walks into the house. I love hearing the dialogue around the dinner table. I love the sound of giggling girls; I try to guess whose footsteps I hear running down the hall. Truth be told, it doesn't bother me too much to hear the sibling rivalry happening.

Having children in my life has given me a deep calling to do what I can to make sure no future generations experience the kind of abuse that I did. I believe that as I heal, I create space for others to heal. When I share my story, I make space for others to share their story. I stay committed to this vision by realizing that I am on a healing journey, not just for myself but also for others. Any time I feel like giving up, I am reminded that healing from my experiences is not a one-and-done situation. My healing journey is like peeling an onion. There is always another layer. I am also reminded that I am not alone on this journey. Asking for support was not easy at first. It took effort to overcome the fear of rejection. During this journey, I have found different ways to forgive. I have found, "forgiveness is for me to choose to hurt and suffer less even though I am wounded." This way of looking at forgiveness works when I am in the moment and I am holding bitterness and anger toward someone who is out of my reach. I actively put my level of pain on a numeric scale from one to ten and figure out what will make me feel better right now. Another tool is my visualization of all of the people who hurt me standing in front of me wanting to be forgiven. First in line is myself. When I am able to forgive myself, I find it much easier to forgive others.

Resilient Living Tips

1. How is your perspective shifting and changing?

2. What is positive and good around you?

3. What can you celebrate, appreciate, and enjoy?

4. How can you choose to hurt less by forgiving yourself and others?

Notes

_____

_____

_____

_____

_____

_____

_____

_____

_____

_____

_____

_____

_____

_____

_____

_____

_____

_____

_____

_____

_____

Notes

_____

_____

_____

_____

_____

_____

_____

_____

_____

_____

_____

_____

_____

_____

_____

_____

_____

_____

_____

_____

_____

_____

_____

CHAPTER FIVE

The Future

"What are you building?"

I am building a resilient life one choice at a time. Sometimes the choice is what to do first thing in the morning. Do I choose to face this day or do I pull the covers over my head and stay in bed? There is a myriad of factors that affect this very choice. Some days I go through it not fully engaged. At the end of a day like this, I should have pulled the covers over my head and stayed in bed because a day spent not fully engaged is wasted. I strive to take steps each day to build what matters to me. What are you choosing to build each day?

"How do you build the life that you want?"

Building the life I want starts with knowing what that life is. I can say at the moment that I have more clarity about the life that I don't want. This is not from uncertainty as much as it is a realization that joy may show up in unexpected ways in life. For example, I was so convinced that having children in my life would not bring me joy. Now I have grandchildren and I experience a level of joy that words cannot express. During my teens and twenties, I had no desire to have children and I tried to build a life that did not include them. While I don't regret the choices I've made at that time, I do wonder how my life would be different. Are you clear on what you want and don't want? Are you aligning your life with what is important to you?

"Are you helping others?"

I will leave it to others to answer if I have helped or if I am helping them or not. As for my efforts to help others, I hope that sharing my story helps others.

My work with Santa Clara County helps. Spending time with my grandchildren helps. How are you choosing to help others?

**"You are not alone/Share your gifts/
Help others with their vision, too."**

I know that I am not alone because I get opportunities to share my gifts. This is where the choices are made. Do I choose to step into that opportunity or do I choose to stay hidden? On a good day, I am willing to shine. I will say that when I saw other people shine, I had the desire to shine as well; however, for me to shine is a process. It took me some time to realize that living resiliently doesn't mean that there is no struggle. Every time I gave in to the struggle, I felt like I was failing to live resiliently. I now know that if I am still breathing, I am living resiliently. So, I can take the next breath and then take one action at a time. Living resiliently actually means continuing to step forward, continuing to rise up, and to live fully and deeply.

The future can be very unpredictable, but I do have hopes and dreams toward which I can take actions. Sharing my story on a larger scale is one place to start. Spending time and energy to uplift others is another option. I choose to continue to step forward, live resiliently and purposefully. You don't need to do it all alone. Bring those people around you to support and cheer you on resiliently ...one step at a time. Know that I am here, cheering you on as you embrace your resilient journey. Every step counts and creates a positive ripple in the world. Keep stepping forward resiliently, purposefully, and with an empowered spring in your step.

A Resilient Dream…

As I consider dreams for the future, two kinds of dreams come to mind, the dreams that occur during sleep and the dreams that propel the actions that one takes during waking hours. My favorite example of this kind of dream comes from a quote by Harriet Tubman. "I had reasoned this out in my mind; there was one of two things I had a right to, liberty or death; if I could not have one, I would have the other; for no man should take me alive, of freedom, keep going." And she kept going. She also made it possible for other slaves to find freedom. Harriet Tubman is such an inspiration and a challenge to me. At a young age, she suffered a severe head injury that caused a disorder that would cause her to fall asleep randomly. My head injury caused diminished eyesight. When I find myself so committed to making the world a better place that I don't consider letting my eyesight challenge stand in my way, I look at the picture of Harriet Tubman and say, 'thank you for your strength and determination.' When I find myself giving into the negativity that will cause me to lose that commitment, I look at her picture and see the challenge of what she faced. It becomes almost impossible to give in, especially when I can almost hear her voice saying, "If you hear the dogs, keep going. If you see the torches in the woods, keep going. If there's shouting after you, keep going. Don't ever stop. Keep going. If you want a taste of freedom, keep going."

The dogs, the torches, and the shouting, as well as the freedom for me, are different for me today than they were for her back then. While these were literal for her, they are metaphors for me. My dream of freedom is to live in a world where there is no longer a need for agencies that handle child abuse. A world free from child abuse happens when every child can live a life full of love, where all their basic needs are met, where they have the freedom to play outside with other children, in order to have their innocence preserved. As I hold this dream, I take the actions during my waking hours to make it come true. Right now, I do it for my three grandchildren. So far so good. I share my experiences of survival so that my story can serve as inspiration to those who need to see an example.

The journey continues and the future is constantly and rapidly changing. As I consider the world in which my grandchildren will grow up, I carry a dream that comes from my deep desire for their life experiences to be free from the ills that my early life consisted of. So far so good. This is no different than any loving grandparent desires for the generations that follow them.

Resilient Living Tips

1. What are you building?

2. What steps can you take to build the life you want?

3. What support do you need to do so and how can you bring that into your life?

4. How are you helping others?

5. How can you support others in living resiliently too?

Notes

_____

_____

_____

_____

_____

_____

_____

_____

_____

_____

_____

_____

_____

_____

_____

_____

_____

_____

_____

_____

_____

Notes

_____

_____

_____

_____

_____

_____

_____

_____

_____

_____

_____

_____

_____

_____

_____

_____

_____

_____

_____

_____

Resilient Living Tips

1. Make a list of any physical scrapes, bumps, and bruises that are still in the healing process. Consider what you may need to do in order to boost the body's ability to continue to heal and take those actions.

2. Is there an action/mindset that you can take on that will help the healing process? Your own "kiss" to make it better? (I'm sending positive energy and support to remind you that you are not alone; your hurts matter and are cared for.)

3. Know that you can choose to turn them into a badge of honor and a testament to what you have survived. A reminder of your RESILIENCE.

1. Look at yourself in the mirror and say: "Today, I love you."

2. You no longer have to stay silent.

3. Choose to heal.

4. Release what does not serve.

5. Embrace your resilience.

1. Stand in your truth.

2. Differences are actually gifts to celebrate and share.

3. Don't "tone yourself down"; in fact, "Tone Yourself Up!"

4. Release the SHAME.

5. Find your purpose and reason to shine!

6. Choose how you define success.

7. Choose to SHINE by sharing how you have healed.

1. How is your perspective shifting and changing?

2. What is positive and good around you?

3. What can you celebrate, appreciate, and enjoy?

4. How can you choose to hurt less by forgiving yourself and others?

1. What are you building?

2. What steps can you take to build the life you want?

3. What support do you need to do so and how can you bring that into your life?

4. How are you helping others?

5. How can you support others in living resiliently too?

About the Author

Kari is the author of *Black, Blind and Female* and a contributing author to the bestselling e-book, *Village Pearls: Spiritual Practices to Uplift Your Soul* and the No. 1 Amazon bestsellers, *Heal Thy Self* and *Step Forward and Shine*. She is also the creator, producer, and performer of her one-woman shows "Somebody Else's Child," "Three Chairs," and "From Garbage to Gold." Kari has presented to and entertained audiences and VIPs at sold-out events all around northern California. She is the subject and star of the documentary, *Gifted Messenger*.

Website: voicesofresilience.com

Email: kari@voicesofresilience.com

Social media

FB: https://www.facebook.com/kari.foxkelley

Twitter: https://twitter.com/Karionk2

Linkedin: https://www.linkedin.com/in/kakelley/

IG: www.instagram.com/resiliencewithkari/

Reviews

"This book is an amazing, inspiring journey, where bitter lemons of life turn into delicious lemonade of life-changing experiences. You will acknowledge it is possible to rise above any situation. This book shows the power in forgiveness, even when life has rejections, and tragic situations. You feel the emotions, the helplessness, and pain of her childhood, as the author learns to cope and adjust. However, the strength, the determination to rise above her circumstances creates a bold, powerful, resilient, and successful woman who can handle anything with God. I recommend this book to anyone who is ready for a life change, and freedom!"

-Toni Stone Bruce, Founder & CEO Precious Stones 4 Life, LLC

Motivational speaker, Best-seller international author, health & wellness consultant Preciousstones4life@gmail.com, tonib.firstfitness.com

"A powerful, beautiful guide on how to build a resilient life, one choice at a time. As an adult survivor of child-hood abuse, Kari Kelley shares her epic story of resilience and devotion to helping children be safe and free from abuse. Kari's compelling voice, testimony and excellent tips for resilient living help readers access their own built-in resilience to "keep going" toward their freedom dreams. Reading Kari's book left me wanting to burst through the pages, and give her a massive hug! Thank you, Kari, for your "strength and determination." You're an inspiration delivering profound encouragement for us all!"

-Marlene Elizabeth, Certified Positive Intelligence® Coach

Moneywings™ Retreats for Entrepreneurs

www.MarleneElizabeth.com

"This book is powerful beyond words. Who doesn't feel sorry for themselves once in a while? We all do, but listening to the hurdles and challenges you have overcome is priceless. I am so happy to hear how you worked through your challenges. Secondly, I like the structure to turn the focus on the reader to analyze their own life. You are sheer amazement. Remember, it is not what others say but how you feel about yourself. You have to know who you are and block out the voices of the critics."

-Rosalyn Kahn, Coaching and Professional Speaking

Host "Living Your Best Life" Chow Entertainment, Best-selling Author, College Professor www.rosalynkahn.com

"Living Resiliently is a heroic story of emerging victorious over odds, narrated in a deeply moving manner. It provides the reader with points to ponder, which can effectively help one in overcoming sorrows.

The author, Kari Kelley—abandoned by her biological parents, abused by foster parents, traumatized by bullying and betrayals in love, and worst of all, blinded by being shaken too hard as an infant—what a life she has lived! Yet, as the phoenix with which she compares herself, she has risen from the ashes to be not only enjoying every moment of her life now, but also actively pursuing her vision to make the world a better place for children! Living Resiliently is a masterpiece that exudes inspiration."

-Atifa Deshamukhya, Certified Life Coach (ICF)

Director, Aspiring Excellence Private Limited

www.comeaspire.net

"Living Resiliently! ~Black, Blind, and Female: The Journey Continues~ is a compelling book that encourages you, as the reader, to live resiliently! The author shares how she recognized that she was living resiliently along the way and gave herself credit. She encourages you to consider your life and how you have come through trials and trauma in the past and can forge forward in the future!"

-Cynthia Stott, International Speech and Confidence Coach, Global Visibility Influencer.
CynthiaStottDTM@gmail.com

"Living Resiliently! Black, Blind, and Female. The title alone prepares the reader for a story of considerable challenges. Kari Kelley does not dwell on the scope and depth of her challenges. Instead, her life's many layers of challenges are revealed in small segments. Each segment provides enough context to demonstrate the specifics of the need for resilience. The situation requiring action is presented quickly and efficiently. The focus to be shifted to specific guidance and recommended actions to begin building the resilience necessary to overcome life's challenges. Kelley's intent is to provide actionable steps to heal and grow stronger, overcoming life's challenges."

-James Adams, Master Photographer

Photographic Craftsman

jamesadamsphotography.com

"From the first sentence, I knew this book was one of spirituality and healing, and I was drawn to that immediately. Using her childhood as the starting point, Kari courageously shared her journey of child abuse and subsequent healing. I saw myself in her story. Others may also see themselves, and her words can guide them to peace at last. Thank you, Kari, for your exquisite sharing that allows us to heal and grow to happiness and joy, while we experience that ever-present upward spiral of positivity."

-Carolyn CJ Jones, Gold-medal-winning Author for Self-help Spirituality, ***The Art of Forgiveness: A Promise of Peace,***

Motivational Speaker, Forgiveness Coach, Registered Nurse, (Ret.) http://carolyncjjoness.com

"This book is an amazing read! Kari Kelley pulled at my heartstrings as she shared her story of the challenges she has faced throughout her life. As a person with a disability, as well as being a survivor of abuse, I could really relate with her story and how resiliency allowed her to overcome these experiences. Sharing our stories is what will allow us to help others and make the world a better place."

-Lydia Norman, Disability Advocate and Public Speaker

https://www.linkedin.com/in/lydianorman

"Kari shows us what it means to be resilient - to clear hurdles, obstacles, difficulties, challenges. We all face them, but how do we deal with them? Go over and around it? Only to find it coming back with a vengeance of its own? This book shows you how to take the 'bull by the horn' and stand up to resolve whatever comes your way. Her Resilient Living Tips open up opportunities for self-reflection to lay the foundation of a life of strength and purpose.

This book is the need of the hour."

-Dr. Mary Thomas, Medical Doctor, Motivational Speaker, International Best-Selling Author

drmarythomas09@gmail.com

Notes

_____

_____

_____

_____

_____

_____

_____

_____

_____

_____

_____

_____

_____

_____

_____

_____

_____

_____

_____

_____

Notes

Notes

_____

_____

_____

_____

_____

_____

_____

_____

_____

_____

_____

_____

_____

_____

_____

_____

_____

_____

_____

_____

Notes

Notes

Notes

Notes

_____

_____

_____

_____

_____

_____

_____

_____

_____

_____

_____

_____

_____

_____

_____

_____

_____

_____

_____

_____

_____

Notes

Notes

_____

_____

_____

_____

_____

_____

_____

_____

_____

_____

_____

_____

_____

_____

_____

_____

_____

_____

_____

_____

_____

Notes

Notes

_____

_____

_____

_____

_____

_____

_____

_____

_____

_____

_____

_____

_____

_____

_____

_____

_____

_____

_____

_____

_____

www.ingramcontent.com/pod-product-compliance
Lightning Source LLC
Chambersburg PA
CBHW060336130626
46553CB00003B/1014